24 HOUR HISTORY

THE ASSASSINATION OF MARTIN LUTHER KING JR.

APRIL 4, 1968

Terry Collins

Heinemann
LIBRARY

Chicago, Illinois

© 2014 Heinemann Library
an imprint of Capstone Global Library, LLC
Chicago, Illinois

To contact Capstone Global Library please phone 800-
747-4992, or visit our Web site www.capstonepub.com

Edited by Adam Miller, Abby Colich, and
    John-Paul Wilkins
Designed by Steve Mead
Original illustrations © Advocate Art 2014
Illustrated by Dante Ginevra
Production by Victoria Fitzgerald
Originated by Capstone Global Library Ltd
Printed and bound in the USA

17 16 15 14 13
10 9 8 7 6 5 4 3 2 1

Library of Congress Cataloging-in-Publication Data
Terry Collins
The Assassination of Dr. Martin Luther King Jr.: April 4,
1968 / Terry Collins.
        pages cm.—(24-Hour History)
    Includes bibliographical references and index.
    ISBN 978-1-4329-9296-5 (hb)—ISBN 978-1-4329-
9302-3 (pb)

    2013935055

Acknowledgments
We would like to thank Steffunni L. Ferreromaddah for
her invaluable help in the preparation of this book.

CONTENTS

Direct quotations are indicated by a yellow background.

Direct quotations appear on the following pages: 5, 6, 7, 8, 9.

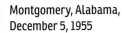

Montgomery, Alabama, December 5, 1955

We are all in agreement of the wrongs done to our dear sister...

Dr. Martin Luther King Jr. agrees to become the president of the Montgomery Improvement Association (MIA).

The association organizes a boycott of all Montgomery buses by the black community to protest what had happened to Rosa Parks four days earlier.

CLEVELAND AV.

We also know things will not change overnight, or in a day, or a week, or a month.

Patience, friends. Patience is our ally here.

Parks was arrested after breaking segregation laws by refusing to give up her seat to a white man.

A response to King's leadership of the association is not long in coming...

On January 30, 1956, King's house is firebombed. Luckily, no one in his family is injured.

King is not frightened into quitting. The assault makes him more determined than ever to see justice done.

I want it to be known the length and breadth of this land that if I am stopped, this movement will not stop.

If I am stopped, our work will not stop. For what we are doing is right.

Montgomery, Alabama, December 21, 1956

The bus boycott ends successfully after 13 months. Blacks ride the buses free of segregation.

Patience is the answer.

But Martin, we had to wait over a year to have the bus companies desegregate seating.

It doesn't matter. If we are calm, and we wait...we shall overcome.

King's patience is rewarded. Following the success of the MIA, King becomes leader of the Southern Christian Leadership Conference (SCLC) in 1957. The organization is formed to coordinate the action of protest groups throughout the South.

On August 28, 1963, King delivers his famous "I Have a Dream" speech. Over 200,000 supporters gather in Washington, D.C., to hear him speak.

I say to you today, my friends, that in spite of the difficulties and frustrations of the moment, I still have a dream.

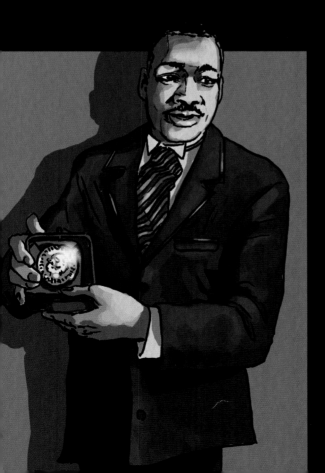

The speech is a passionate cry for justice during the civil rights movement's March on Washington for Jobs and Freedom.

A PRIZE FOR PEACE

On December 10, 1964, Dr. King receives the Nobel Peace Prize in Oslo, Norway. The award recognizes his efforts to use nonviolent means to end segregation and racial discrimination. Gunnar Jahn, Chairman of the Nobel Committee, notes:

"Today we pay tribute to Martin Luther King, the man who has never abandoned his faith in the unarmed struggle he is waging, who has suffered for his faith, who has been imprisoned on many occasions, whose home has been subject to bomb attacks, whose life and the lives of his family have been threatened, and who nevertheless has never faltered."

We've got some difficult days ahead. But it doesn't matter with me now, because I've been to the mountaintop....
Like anybody, I would like to live a long life....But I'm not concerned about that now. I just want to do God's will.
And He's allowed me to go up to the mountain...and I've seen the Promised Land.
I may not get there with you. But I want you to know tonight, that we, as a people, will get to the Promised Land.

10:37 P.M.
The speech over, King leaves the temple for a late night meal.
Can you believe so many came out tonight in this weather, Ralph?
Perhaps Memphis will see our side at last.
His best friend, Ralph Abernathy, is cheered by King's celebratory mood.
They came to see **you**, Martin. The strike is secondary.
Well, we're going to demonstrate for the striking workers, regardless of any federal injunctions saying we can't.
We stand on the First Amendment. We've broken injunctions before, and if necessary, we may do it in Memphis.
Tomorrow will be a long day, my friend. But I'm ready to fight for the right to march again in Memphis.

STRIKE!

On February 12, 1968, over 1,000 black sanitation workers went on strike in the city of Memphis, Tennessee. The men took a stand for better working conditions. They protested low wages, few or no benefits, and racial slurs from white supervisors. When the city refused to negotiate, Dr. King was asked to lend his support.

On March 18, King made a personal appearance and spoke in Memphis. He returned on March 28 to lead a march down Beale Street for the striking workers. To his horror, violence erupted. Windows were broken and stores were looted. When police arrived, marchers threw stones. Authorities responded with tear gas. At least one marcher was shot.

King was deeply troubled by these events during a march under his leadership. He quickly scheduled another march on April 8. However, the city of Memphis used the power of the federal government to refuse King permission to stage his demonstration. Ironically, the main reason for this federal injunction was fear for King's safety.

"A SHADOW CAST"

New Rebel Motel Restaurant, April 4, 1968

10:14 A.M.

Escaped convict James Earl Ray, traveling under the alias of Eric S. Galt, reads one of the local Memphis newspapers.

Something catches Ray's eye on the front page...

A local reporter carelessly reveals the exact location where the visiting Dr. King is staying...

...the Lorraine Motel. Room number 306 is clearly visible in the photograph.

11:23 A.M.

Ray makes a quick call to his brother, Jerry.

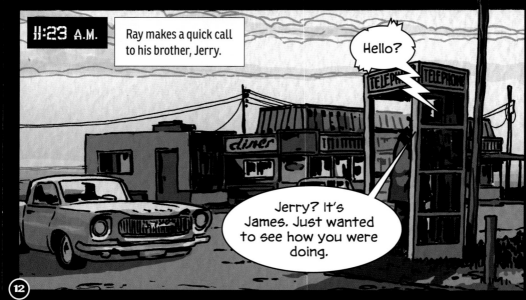

Hello?

Jerry? It's James. Just wanted to see how you were doing.

What, a man can't call his own brother?
Right. Well, soon it will be all over. I might not see you for a while.
Don't worry about me. I'll be all right.

*Andrew Young: Young was a close friend of King and a fellow member of the SCLC. He attended the court hearing with King's lawyer, Chauncey Eskridge.

Got any vacancies?

James Earl Ray, knowing where King was staying, had discovered an interesting fact...

We've got six rooms.

This is our nicest one.

No, I don't need a kitchen. Have you got a smaller room?

I only want a bed for sleeping.
One bed for sleeping. You share the bathroom at the end of the hall.
...the rooms at the back of the boardinghouse looked out directly at the Lorraine Motel.
All Ray needed was a direct line of sight through a window.
This one's $8.50 for the week.
Yeah, this is fine.
This'll do just fine.

The judge listened to eight hours of testimony, but finally agreed to modify the injunction.
As long as everything is tightly controlled, and planned out to avoid surprises, we're golden.

The march is back on.
Then we've won.
We've won!

A "DANGEROUS UNSELFISHNESS"

5:02 P.M. Parked near the boardinghouse, Ray waits for local traffic to clear.

Privacy is required to retrieve his deadly luggage from the trunk of his car.

Hidden in the green blanket is a new Remington Gamemaster Model 760 rifle.

5:38 P.M.
King gets ready for dinner. He is due to eat at the home of Reverend Billy Kyles.
Ralph, call and see what's on the menu tonight.
Billy's wife says roast beef, candied yams, pig's feet, neck bones, chitlins, turnip greens, and corn pone.
KNOCK KNOCK
I bet that's Billy now.

5:55 P.M.

Back at the boardinghouse, James Earl Ray perches on a hard wooden chair.

He watches and waits.

He has seen visitors to King's room, but no sign of the man himself.

But then, to Ray's surprise...

...his quarry unsuspectingly reveals himself.

As good as the view from his room is, using a weapon there is not possible. To get a line of sight to shoot at King, Ray needs a better angle.

Such an angle is available from the window of the communal bathroom at the end of the hall.

The Remington Gamemaster is a powerful weapon; overkill, really, for the task at hand.

The Lorraine Motel

Behind the wheel of a white Cadillac, Dr. King's driver, Solomon Jones, starts the engine.

Jesse Jackson, another member of King's team, and Ben Branch, a local Memphis singer, greet Dr. King.

This is Ben Branch. He's with the band playing tonight at the benefit for the striking workers.

Good to see you, Doc.

Ben, I want you to sing for me tonight at the meeting.
Do that song, "Take My Hand, Precious Lord."
Doc, it's getting chilly! I think you'll need a topcoat.
Okay, Jonesy! You really know how to take good care of me.

What thoughts go through the head of an assassin as he tracks his prey?

What is Ray thinking as he loads his rifle with soft-pointed bullets, designed to cause maximum damage to a victim?

The dark corridors of Ray's mind remain private.

CLICK

Ray takes a deep breath and pulls the trigger.

A single bullet smashes through the air at a speed of 2,670 feet (814 meters) per second.

A single bullet is all that is required to topple a leader of men.

A single bullet.

Hey! Did you hear that noise?

6:15 P.M.

St. Joseph Hospital. Despite the heroic efforts of the doctors, King's injuries are too serious for him to be saved.

7:05 P.M.

Dr. Martin Luther King Jr., never regains consciousness. He dies that night at 7:05 p.m. But his legacy lives on.

CONCLUSION: THE DREAM ENDURES

Dr. Martin Luther King Jr., died on April 4, 1968, at the tragically young age of 39. The civil rights movement lost not only a leader, but also the voice of a generation. However, King's work continued after his passing, with his friends and followers taking up the torch for equal rights for all citizens. His close friend, Ralph Abernathy, stepped into King's role as the president of the Southern Christian Leadership Conference (SCLC). He led a peaceful demonstration down the streets of Memphis on April 8 as planned. A pall of mourning hung over the marchers, but so did a sense of determination that King's work was not finished and would not die with him.

President Lyndon B. Johnson said upon learning of King's assassination: "We can achieve nothing by lawlessness and divisiveness among the American people. It is only by joining together and only by working together that we can continue to move toward equality and fulfillment for all of our people." Johnson was a longtime supporter of civil rights and signer of the Civil Rights Act of 1964, which prohibited discrimination of all kinds based on race, color, religion, or national origin. He knew that once grieving for the fallen leader was over, two things would occur. One of them would be the continuing progress of the civil rights movement. The other would be a thirst for justice in the capture of King's killer.

A degree of closure would come with the capture and conviction of James Earl Ray, the shooter who robbed the world of King's presence. An escaped convict with a series of previous stays in prison, Ray remained at large for months. As investigators pieced together the evidence Ray left behind, they knew who their quarry was. The only thing left was to find the assassin and let him stand trial.

Ray was arrested, tried, and sentenced for his crime. Dr. Martin Luther King's murderer would spend the rest of his life in prison, watching as King's legacy lived on. He died in prison on April 23, 1998.

Just days after King's death, President Johnson signed the Civil Rights Act of 1968, prohibiting discrimination in the sale, rent, and financing of housing. The Act further demonstrated Johnson's commitment to civil rights, and his determination to achieve something significant on behalf of King's legacy. In 1971 the Supreme Court upheld busing as a legitimate way to achieve integration of public schools. As recently as 1991, another Civil Rights Act was signed by then president George H. W. Bush to strengthen civil rights laws and provide for damages in cases of intentional employment discrimination.

Dr. Martin Luther King Jr.'s legacy still lives on today.

TIMELINE

February 1, 1968	Memphis, Tennessee. Sanitation workers Robert Walker and Echol Cole are both killed in a horrific garbage truck accident when the trash compactor malfunctions.
February 12, 1968	Over 1,000 black employees from the Memphis Public Works department go on strike due to substandard working conditions, including safety issues
March 18, 1968	King speaks to a crowd of over 15,000 supporters of the strike in Memphis, and agrees to lead a protest march
March 28, 1968	The march erupts in violence, shocking King and drawing strong criticism of the striking workers. King vows to return to Memphis for a second protest march.

April 3, 1968

10:55 a.m.	King and his staff arrive by jet in Memphis and check into the Lorraine Motel
1:00 p.m.	Word of a federal injunction against any demonstration led by King is received. The court says there will be no march.
9:00 p.m.	King makes an impassioned speech at the Mason Temple and renews his pledge to lead a second march

April 4, 1968

8:00 a.m.–4:00 p.m.	King spends the day at the Lorraine Motel, holding meetings and waiting for word from the court about the injunction
3:25 p.m.	James Earl Ray takes a room at Bessie Brewer's boardinghouse
4:06 p.m.	Ray purchases a set of binoculars to monitor King at the Lorraine Motel
5:00 p.m.	King receives good news. The U.S. District Court has agreed to allow a tightly controlled march on April 8.

The times given in this book are approximate and may vary between sources.

5:10 p.m.	James Earl Ray starts his surveillance of the door of King's room through his binoculars, waiting for his target to emerge
5:55 p.m.	Gathering with a group of his staff, King prepares to leave the Lorraine Motel for a dinner at the home of a local minister. He stops on the balcony outside his room to talk to his driver, who is waiting down below.
6:01 p.m.	Ray takes aim and fires a single shot, striking King in the upper jaw and damaging his jugular vein and windpipe. The bullet travels downward, cutting King's spinal cord.
6:02 p.m.	Fleeing the boardinghouse, Ray leaves the murder weapon behind in a doorway on the street before leaving the scene in a white Ford Mustang
6:09 p.m.	The mortally wounded King is carried by ambulance to St. Joseph Hospital
7:05 p.m.	Dr. Martin Luther King Jr. is pronounced dead at St. Joseph Hospital
April 5, 1968	President Lyndon B. Johnson declares April 7 as a national day of mourning
April 8, 1968	The planned march through Memphis goes on as scheduled, now in memorial of the slain King
April 9, 1968	More than 50,000 people accompany King's coffin through Atlanta, Georgia, to its final resting place at South View Cemetery
June 8, 1968	Ray, under a variety of aliases, has remained at large, but is finally arrested in London, England, at Heathrow Airport
July 19, 1968	An extradited James Earl Ray arrives in Memphis to stand trial for the assassination of Dr. King
March 10, 1969	Ray pleads guilty to killing King, and receives a life sentence of 99 years in Brushy Mountain State Penitentiary in Tennessee
April 23, 1998	James Earl Ray dies in prison at the age of 70

CAST OF CHARACTERS

Ralph Abernathy (1926–1990)
King's best friend and second in command of the Southern Christian Leadership Conference (SCLC), Abernathy was born in Linden, Alabama, on March 11, 1926. A World War II veteran, Abernathy graduated from Alabama State University with a degree in mathematics in 1950 and an MA in sociology from Atlanta University in 1951. He became the pastor of the First Baptist Church in Montgomery, Alabama, where he first met King. After King's tragic shooting, Abernathy accompanied his friend in the ambulance to St. Joseph's Hospital. He succeeded him as SCLC president and continued King's philosophy of using nonviolent resistance to achieve equality for African Americans. Abernathy died in Atlanta on April 17, 1990.

Jesse Jackson (b. 1941)
Born on October 8, 1941, in Greenville, South Carolina, Jackson was a member of King's staff and witnessed the shooting of his friend and leader at the Lorraine Hotel. A powerful speaker and Baptist preacher, Jackson has never stopped working for the rights of minorities. He campaigned as a Democratic presidential nominee in both the 1984 and 1988 elections, and went on to assist in the release of several U.S. hostages held internationally. In 1989, Jackson received the Spingarn Medal from the National Association for the Advancement of Colored People (NAACP) for outstanding achievement by an African American. The award was presented for Jackson's lifetime achievements in civil rights.

Dr. Martin Luther King Jr. (1929–1968)
King was born in Atlanta, Georgia, on January 15, 1929. Both his father and grandfather were Baptist preachers, and Martin followed in the family tradition. He attended Morehouse College and Crozer Theological Seminary and received his doctorate of theology from Boston University. King was later influenced by the peaceful teachings of Gandhi and the philosophy of civil disobedience through nonviolent protest. Thanks to his powerful intellect and charismatic speaking skills, he became the unofficial leader of the civil rights movement. His words and passion led to the March on Washington to highlight the need for civil rights. On August 28, 1963, over 200,000 people gathered at the Lincoln Memorial to hear King's "I Have a Dream" speech. He was awarded the Nobel Peace Prize in 1964.

James Earl Ray (1928–1998)

One of eight children, Ray was a mediocre student and failed member of the U.S. Army before he turned to crime. Born on March 10, 1928, in Alton, Illinois, his family was extremely poor. After leaving the armed forces, Ray worked several dead-end jobs before moving to Los Angeles, California, in 1949, where he was promptly arrested for burglary. A series of arrests for mail fraud and armed robbery followed throughout the 1950s, until he was sentenced to 20 years for armed robbery in 1959. Ray escaped in 1967 and traveled throughout North America under a series of aliases until he assassinated Dr. Martin Luther King Jr. Ray's reasons for the murder remain unclear, other than racial hatred and possible recognition for such a high-profile killing. Sentenced to 99 years, Ray died in prison on April 23, 1998, at age 70.

Andrew Young (b. 1932)

The accomplishments of Andrew Young are many. Born March 12, 1932, in New Orleans, Louisiana, Young went on to serve as one of King's chief aides and the executive director of the SCLC from 1964 to 1970. A graduate of Howard University and Hartford Theological Seminary, he was ordained a minister in 1955. After his time with the SCLC, he represented the state of Georgia in the U.S. House of Representatives in 1972, leaving only to become the U.S. Ambassador to the United Nations in 1978. After resigning from this post in 1979, Young was elected Mayor of Atlanta, Georgia, in 1981, where he served for two successful terms. He continues to write and speak about world politics and civil rights.

GLOSSARY

aide person who gives support on something

alias made-up name

association group of people who have joined together for a common cause

communal belonging to members of a community

cosmic relating to the universe

creed set of beliefs held by a person or group

discrimination unfair treatment of people because of their skin color, sex, or personal beliefs

equality condition of being equal

extradite transfer a person accused of a crime from one state or country to the country in which the crime was committed

falter become unsure or unsteady; hesitate

infrared form of technology that uses invisible bands of radiation, enabling the user to see in the dark

injunction order from a court to stop someone from doing something

musing deep thought or reflection on something

patience ability to stay calm and wait

perception ability to see, hear, or become aware of something through the senses

quarry living creature that is being hunted

segregation practice of separating people into groups, especially by race

slur negative remark

FIND OUT MORE

Books

Bausum, Ann. *Marching to the Mountaintop: How Poverty, Labor Fights, and Civil Rights Set the Stage for Martin Luther King Jr.'s Final Hours.* Washington, D.C.: National Geographic, 2012.

Jazynka, Kitson. *Martin Luther King, Jr. (Readers Bios).* Washington, D.C.: National Geographic, 2012.

King, Martin Luther, Jr. *I Have Dream.* New York: Schwartz and Wade, 2012.

Myers, Walter Dean. *I've Seen the Promised Land: The Life of Dr. Martin Luther King, Jr.* New York: Amistad, 2012.

DVDs

Citizen King: American Experience, PBS Home Video, 2004.

In Remembrance of Martin, PBS Home Video, 1998.

King: A Filmed Record; Montgomery to Memphis, Kino Lorber, 1970.

Martin Luther King, Jr.: The Man and the Dream, A&E Home Video, 2004.

Who Killed Martin Luther King?, Clarendon Entertainment, 2008.

Web Sites

www.archives.gov/research/jfk/select-committee-report/part-2a.html
A report of the Select Committee on Assassinations of the U.S. House of Representatives regarding the King Assassination. Its findings, interviews, and collected evidence concur that James Earl Ray fired a single shot and killed Dr. King.

crdl.usg.edu/events/mlk_assassination
A page with letters, legal documents, photographs, sound recordings, FBI files, oral histories, and historical news clips about the assassination and the aftermath.

www.history.com/topics/martin-luther-king-assassination
A collection maintained by The History Channel featuring a photo gallery, video clips, an interactive timeline, speeches, and much more. An excellent starting point for anyone interested in learning more about King's death.

www.thekingcenter.org
The King Center features an extensive online collection of the works and papers of Dr. King. The Web site was introduced in 2011, and the goal is to eventually digitize more than one million documents, with new content being added regularly from the King Center Archive collection.

Places to Visit

Martin Luther King, Jr. National Historic Site
450 Auburn Avenue, NE
Atlanta, GA 30312-1525
404-331-5190
Visitors Information: 404-331-6922 (recording)
www.nps.gov/malu

Martin Luther King, Jr., National Memorial
900 Ohio Drive SW
Washington, DC 20024
202-426 6841
www.nps.gov/mlkm/index.htm

National Civil Rights Museum at the Lorraine Motel
450 Mulberry Street
Memphis, TN 38103
901-521-9699
www.civilrightsmuseum.org

INDEX